Looking at . . . Coelophysis

A Dinosaur from the TRIASSIC Period

THE NEW
DINOSAUR
COLLECTION

For a free color catalog describing Gareth Stevens' list of high-quality books, call 1-800-542-2595 (USA) or 1-800-461-9120 (Canada). Gareth Stevens' Fax: (414) 225-0377.

Library of Congress Cataloging-in-Publication Data

Coleman, Graham, 1963-
   Looking at-- Coelophysis / written by Graham Coleman; illustrated by Tony Gibbons.
      p. cm. -- (The New dinosaur collection)
   Includes index.
   ISBN 0-8368-1139-9
   1. Coelophysis--Juvenile literature. [1. Coelophysis. 2. Dinosaurs.] I. Gibbons, Tony, ill.
II. Title. III. Series.
QE862.S3C63 1994
567.9'7--dc20
                                    94-11524

This North American edition first published in 1994 by
Gareth Stevens Publishing
1555 North RiverCenter Drive, Suite 201
Milwaukee, Wisconsin 53212 USA

This U.S. edition © 1994 by Gareth Stevens, Inc. Created with original © 1994 by
Quartz Editorial Services, Premier House, 112 Station Road, Edgware HA8 7AQ U.K.

Consultant: Dr. David Norman, Director of the Sedgwick Museum of Geology,
University of Cambridge, England.

Additional artwork by Clare Herronneau.

Printed in the United States of America

 2 3 4 5 6 7 8 9 99 98 97 96 95

Looking at . . .
Coelophysis
A Dinosaur from the TRIASSIC Period

by Graham Coleman

Illustrated by Tony Gibbons

THE NEW
DINOSAUR
COLLECTION

Gareth Stevens Publishing
MILWAUKEE

Contents

Introducing Coelophysis

One of the very first dinosaurs, **Coelophysis** (SEE-LOW-FI-SIS) was small and spindly, roaming those parts of the world we now know as North America, Europe, South Africa, and South America. It lived about 210 million years ago during Triassic times.

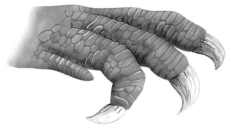

Just look at those claws! **Coelophysis** used them for catching small prey, which it would then tear apart for a meal.

The remains of **Coelophysis** were first dug up in the last century in New Mexico. Some of the skeletons unearthed later are among the most perfect dinosaur skeletons we have yet found.

Coelophysis was a lightly built creature and had a long neck that ended in a thin head. One of the strangest things about this dinosaur was its skull, which was full of holes.

But how did **Coelophysis** live? And how do scientists know what it looked like?

Turn the pages that follow and find out all about this fascinating prehistoric creature. You are about to discover that this dinosaur was actually a cannibal, eating the young of its own kind!

Small but fearsome

Perhaps you think that **Coelophysis** might have been fun to get to know.

Coelophysis was about 10 feet (3 meters) long. Much of its body consisted of tail and neck.

You can see in the picture how **Coelophysis** would compare in size with a human being. **Coelophysis** was small by dinosaur standards. But even though it was not a giant, it was a greedy meat-eater and would attack for food. So if it were around today, you would need to beware! It would not make an ideal pet.

A fully grown adult **Coelophysis** probably weighed about 65 pounds (30 kilograms).

Take a look at **Coelophysis** as it is shown here, running. It sprinted on slim back legs, so that its shorter front limbs were left free for the business of grabbing at prey such as insects, lizards, or other creatures, including small dinosaurs.

When **Coelophysis** was hungry, those clawed hands came in very useful!

It loved to feed on dragonflies. Our artist has imagined that if **Coelophysis** had survived to present times, it might have mistaken this boy's remote control airplane for a dragonfly.

Coelophysis had a long, pointed head and large eyes.

No one knows for certain what color **Coelophysis** was. Fossilized dinosaur skin loses its color over millions of years. Artists and model-makers therefore have to guess.

There are, however, quite a lot of other facts that paleontologists (scientists studying fossilized remains) have discovered about **Coelophysis**.

Lightweight skeleton

When scientists first put together the bones they had dug up from **Coelophysis**'s skeleton, they saw that it had been a very lightly built dinosaur.

Its jaws were long and narrow, ideal for trapping winged insects, and contained a number of small, but razor-sharp, teeth. These were perfect for slicing meat and made **Coelophysis** a dangerous predator.

Coelophysis's skull was also light and had several holes, or "windows," in it. (The bones of birds have similar hollow spaces inside them.) **Coelophysis** did not have a lot of weight to carry and so would have been able to run very fast.

Three of the four fingers on **Coelophysis**'s front limbs were long and well designed for grabbing and holding, but the fourth was rather useless.

Look how long and thin its tail was! **Coelophysis** used its tail to help it balance as it ran at great speed through the Triassic landscape.

Coelophysis's back legs were far longer than its front limbs, and its three-toed feet were similar in some ways to those of birds.

Most scientists now think that birds probably evolved from early dinosaurs.

This all points toward the possibility of some sort of link between early dinosaurs and birds. You might have thought that birds evolved from pterosaurs, the flying reptiles of prehistoric times. But this is not generally thought to be the case.

So what are the main features you need to look for in order to tell the skeleton of a **Coelophysis** from that of other dinosaurs? Here are the points to check.

Birds, of course, do not have teeth, like dinosaurs did.

But dinosaurs did lay eggs, just as birds do. And the bone structure of birds and dinosaurs is quite similar.

- Does it have a slim body with long jaws?
- Is there a long, thin tail that is slimmer toward the end?
- Are there strong claws on three of its four fingers?
- Can you spot a flexible neck and sharp teeth?

If so, then the chances are that it is indeed a **Coelophysis**, or one of its close relatives. What a wonderful creature!

9

In Late Triassic

Some scientists believe the world looked very different when dinosaurs first evolved. There was just one huge continent. You could have walked all over the land on Earth without having to cross its seas.

But there were early signs of the landmasses beginning to split up and forming the continents we have today. Vegetation was very different then, too. There was no grass, and no flowering plants had appeared yet.

times

Ferns and horsetails grew by the water, and there were tall conifers. Dinosaurs ranged from rabbit-size to **Coelophysis**-size. In some places, there were also large, plant-eating dinosaurs.

Discovery at

The first remains of **Coelophysis** were discovered by an American scientist named David Baldwin over a hundred years ago. He found some bones in Triassic rocks at a place called Ghost Ranch in New Mexico. They were an incredible 210 million years old! Baldwin had once helped the well-known dinosaur paleontologist, O. C. Marsh, but later worked for his great rival, the famous bone hunter, Edward Drinker Cope. It was Cope who gave the dinosaur **Coelophysis** its name, meaning "hollow form." This referred to the holes in its bones.

To begin with, very little was known about the creature. The remains that had been found did not make up a whole skeleton. Cope thought there were three types of

Ghost Ranch

Coelophysis, but he was later proved wrong. He had mistaken three **Coelophysis** of three different sizes and ages for three different species.

Sixty years later, scientists from the American Museum of Natural History went back to where **Coelophysis** had first been discovered. They thought there might be more dinosaur bones to find there – and they were right!

They dug into the hillside and now found lots of complete skeletons of **Coelophysis** – possibly as many as one hundred. There were babies as well as adults, and it seemed they had all died at the same time for some mysterious reason.

Cannibals!

Coelophysis was one of the first dinosaurs ever to appear on planet Earth. It is also the oldest dinosaur that scientists know well. This is mainly due to the large number of skeletons dug up at Ghost Ranch in 1947. Many hundreds of bones were found there.

Scientists were amazed to find the bones of baby **Coelophysis** inside the rib cages of some of the adult **Coelophysis**. At first, they thought the bones belonged to babies developing inside the mother **Coelophysis**.

But the most shocking discovery made at Ghost Ranch was that **Coelophysis** was a cannibal – an animal that eats its own kind.

But the bones were too big for that. Scientists also now know that all dinosaurs laid eggs and did not give birth to live young, as mammals do.

So what could have driven these dinosaurs to eat their own kind? Did it happen often?

Or were these dinosaur cannibals starving creatures that were desperate for any food they could find? Whatever the answer to this mystery, it was probably the last meal these dinosaurs ever ate. Not long afterward, the cannibals – along with dozens of other **Coelophysis** – met their death in some prehistoric disaster.

Hunting in packs

Heterodontosaurus
(<u>HET</u>-ER-OH-<u>DONT</u>-OH-<u>SAW</u>-RUS) was nibbling at some plants. It was a small herbivore, only about the size of a family dog. It cut off some leaves with its sharp front teeth and used its large cheek teeth to grind up its meal. Little did **Heterodontosaurus** know that its life was in terrible danger.

A pack of **Coelophysis** was on the prowl. They hadn't eaten for hours and were very hungry. If they didn't find something to eat soon, they might even gang up on the weakest member of the pack and eat it! These were cannibals, remember, with little respect for their own kind.

Suddenly, one of them spotted **Heterodontosaurus** and let out a screech of excitement. The first **Coelophysis** ran toward **Heterodontosaurus**, who was slow to realize what was happening. It looked up. Terrified, it found itself face-to-face with a very fierce-looking creature.

These two **Coelophysis** fell to the ground, their fingers digging into each other's flesh while they snapped with their jaws. Behind them, two other **Coelophysis** fell over in the panic. They snarled at each other and also started fighting.

Just as this **Coelophysis** was about to pounce, it was pulled back. One of the other **Coelophysis** was trying to push it out of the way. The greedy creature was starving and wanted a meal of **Heterodontosaurus** all to itself!

Heterodontosaurus saw its chance to escape! It was a fast mover and took off on its back legs, running like the wind. It held its tail out behind it for balance as it dashed for freedom. **Heterodontosaurus** had survived this time – thanks to the greed of the pack of **Coelophysis**.

17

Attack and counterattack

Predatory dinosaurs – those that chased unfortunate prey for food – had different ways of attacking their victims.

Coelophysis (1) was fast on its feet and would run around, trying to grab at its next meal with its terrible clawed fingers. Or it would simply snap up smaller creatures – such as lizards or insects – with its long jaws and sharp teeth.

A giant carnivore such as **Tyrannosaurus rex** (TIE-<u>RAN</u>-OH-<u>SAW</u>-RUS-RECKS) (2), however, would have been more stealthy in its approach, creeping up and then risking an attack against large victims. It would tear chunks of meat from their bodies, even while they were still alive.

3

Ankylosaurus (<u>AN</u>-KY-LO-<u>SAW</u>-RUS) (**4**), shown at the bottom of this page, had a wonderful bony club at the end of its tail with which it could bash an enemy. One whack with this dreadful weapon would have scared off any other dinosaur threatening to attack.

The pointed spikes on its back were also a type of armor, protecting its soft underbelly.

5

Some dinosaurs were particularly lucky. Their bodies helped them make a counterattack when predators threatened.

Iguanodon (IG-<u>WA</u>-NO-DON) (**3**), for instance, had a magnificent thumb spike with which it could stab when necessary.

Other dinosaurs – such as **Gallimimus** (<u>GAL</u>-IH-<u>MIME</u>-US) (**5**) – could not put up much of a fight but had to rely on being speedy runners in order to escape from attack.

4

19

Coelophysis data

Coelophysis had much in common with thecodonts (THEK-OH-DONTS), the crocodilelike creatures that were its ancestors.

Some of these animals originally lived in marshy areas; but, as the climate grew warmer and drier, they came to live more and more on dry land. This meant that they started to walk more easily with their legs swinging under their bodies.

Some also began to use their front limbs for catching prey. All this, of course, took millions of years, but eventually Coelophysis evolved.

Snakelike neck
Coelophysis's neck was fairly long and slender. It is likely to have been quite flexible, so Coelophysis could shake its prey from side to side when tearing into it.

Narrow head
Its head was small but long and consisted mostly of narrow jaws. Scientists think Coelophysis may have been an intelligent dinosaur. Its fairly large brain meant that it had good coordination of hand and eye, which made it a successful hunter.

Skull windows

Small, lightly built dinosaurs, such as **Coelophysis,** often had holes (scientists call them *fenestrae,* meaning "windows") in their skulls. This left a lot of room for muscles, giving them strong jaws. But it also meant that they had to be very careful if attacked.

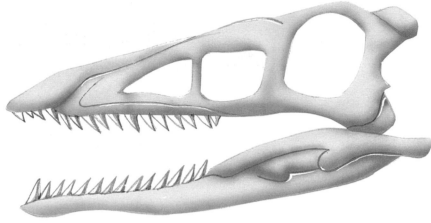

Fearsome fingers

Coelophysis had fairly strong front limbs and used its hands to hold on to its prey. Each hand had four fingers, one of which was very small and hardly used at all. The other three fingers were long, with curved claws. **Coelophysis** was probably quite vicious with its claws when hunting for food.

There was little to protect their heads from being crushed by an enemy.

Saw-edged teeth

Coelophysis's teeth had sharp, sawlike edges and they curved backward, as shown above. Its jaws were strong and well suited to slicing the flesh of its prey.

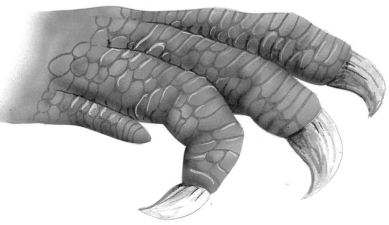

21

The Coelurosaur gang

Coelophysis (**1**) was a **Theropod** (<u>THER</u>-OH-POD). These dinosaurs were all carnivores (meat-eaters), and they existed from the beginning to the end of the age of the dinosaurs.

Within the **Theropod** group, **Coelophysis** is part of a smaller group known as **Coelurosaurs** (SEEL-<u>OO</u>-ROE-SAWRS) or "hollow tail lizards."

Coelurosaurs were similar dinosaurs that lived during the same time but in different parts of the world. In Triassic times, remember, the world was still mostly one large landmass surrounded by sea.

Syntarsus (SIN-TAR-SUS) **(2)** was a two-legged meat-eater whose remains were found in what is now Zimbabwe in Africa. It had strong back legs and arms with just three strong, clawed fingers. It grew up to 10 feet (3 m) long and had a name meaning "fused ankle" because its ankle bones were joined together, unlike those of **Coelophysis**.

Halticosaurus (HAL-TIK-OH-SAW-RUS) **(3)** – its name means "springing reptile" – also lived about 220 million years ago in what is now Germany. It was larger than **Coelophysis** – up to 18 feet (5.5 m) long – and had five fingers on each hand.

Halticosaurus lived side by side with **Procompsognathus** (PRO-COMP-SOG-NAY-THUS) **(4)** – a tiny dinosaur, only 4 feet (1.2 m) long with large eyes and sharp teeth.

Segisaurus (SEG-IH-SAW-RUS) **(5)** lived in North America and was also small – about the size of a goose – with sharp claws on its hands, long legs for its height, and birdlike feet. Unlike **Coelophysis**, its bones were solid, not hollow.

2

4

GLOSSARY

carnivores — meat-eating animals.

conifers — woody shrubs or trees that bear their seeds in cones.

continents — the major landmasses of Earth. Africa, Asia, Australia, Europe, North America, South America, and Antarctica are continents.

evolve — to change shape or develop gradually over a long period of time.

fossils — traces or remains of plants and animals found in rock.

herbivores — plant-eating animals.

predators — animals that kill other animals for food.

prey — animals that are captured and killed for food by other animals.

remains — a skeleton, bones, or a dead body.

skeleton — the bony framework of a body.

INDEX